How Not to Be an A-Hole Wife and Lose Your Husband (A Ridiculously Easy 30-Day Guide)

by Brian Ronalds
edited by Anne-Marie Pritchett

Forward:

Women! This should be a breeze for you! Why? Three words: Men are simple. We really are, and we don't ask for all that much. More than likely, you grabbed this ridiculously easy 30-day guide to smooth things over after you handed him the first book in the series, *How Not to Be an A-Hole Husband and Lose Your Wife*! Let me guess, the first words out of his mouth were, "Where the hell's the women's version?" or "Screw you, woman. I'm not an A-hole!" Sound familiar? So, here you go. You're welcome. Also, there are those women out there that are in dire need for this refresher. They treat their men so poorly and don't even realize it. They embarrass them and belittle them privately AND publically to the point that their men simply just shut down. They stop fighting and throw in the towel. You know who you are girls. You sincerely believe that you can do no wrong! Guess what? It's time to get your head examined, look in the mirror and face the truth with dignity!

As you may or may not know, the average consumer is accustomed to receiving their news in 140 characters or less and watching videos no more than 10 minutes in length. So, I'm going to do just that—keep it short, simple and ridiculously easy to implement. Believe me, as I mentioned in Book One, as much as you don't want to read a 500-page book on how to be the perfect princess, I sure as shit don't want to write one!

In reading this book, I'm most certainly not claiming that I'm uncovering anything groundbreaking or something you've never heard before, but this will be a great reminder on how to treat your man. Believe me, I know, it's hard to change. But it is possible and with time and effort, your man will check back in mentally and provide you with the love, time and energy that he once did before you treated him like an A-hole wife. You owe it to him, but more importantly, you owe it to yourself. At the end of the day, if you're done with your marriage, you're done. But you need to tell him first before running off with a home wrecker who you believe will make everything better! Not true ladies, it only makes things worse. You can keep running away from your problems, but what you can't do is run away from yourself.

If you're reading this, you probably already know you screwed up and are indeed an A-hole wife. You realize now that there are several changes to be made because you love your man and you want to be his best friend, lover and lifelong partner. It's time to look back to when you first met him. His laugh, his smile, the way he made you feel. So, listen up! If he hasn't left yet, then it's not too late. Let me help save you from the most agonizing pain your delicate heart could ever feel. This couldn't be any easier for fuck's sake. Read one page a day for the next 30 days, and remedy the heartache before there is any! It's really not that difficult. In fact, it's ridiculously easy.

Day 1
Don't Be an A-Hole

I would like to congratulate you. Well done! Like anything else, step numero uno is the toughest step to take. You realize that you're an A-hole wife and you want to change. Maybe you don't realize it yet, but you see your man fading away and don't know why. He stops complimenting you and sharing special moments with you and starts finding new ways to occupy his time to do anything but be succumbed to your cruelty and disrespect. Have you taken away his manhood so badly that he's cautious in speaking up to you for fear you might verbally cut his nuts off in front of your friends, family or, even worse, strangers? Knock that shit off, girls! You're making your knight in shining armor feel like a pussy and, in turn, making yourself the A-hole wife. Over the next 30 days, we'll examine the crucial changes necessary to avoid losing your hubby as well as putting plans into action.

So let's do this! We'll keep it simple on Day 1, because on this special day we finally realize it's time for change.

Day 2
Thank Him

Let me ask you something—do you respect your husband? Do you see all that he does for you and your family? Or is it expected? Fuck yes, it's expected! It's easy to start demanding things from your man! Do you expect that he'll bring home a paycheck? That he'll love you? That he'll listen to you? That he'll take you out for a date night, and do you expect that he'll adore you? Guess what…when we expect, demand or require something from somebody, they'll let you down. Every damn time! How cool would it be if you had zero expectations but just completely appreciate what he does for you as a husband? Be super cool, right? Don't get me wrong, there are definitely things that must happen on a day-to-day basis, but appreciate those things. You want to be adored, and he wants to be respected. Tonight, tell him thank you. Thank you for providing, thank him for loving you. You might just freak him the fuck out! Because the truth is, nobody has to do anything; but this "nobody" has promised to spend the rest of his life with you, so respect him or let him go to somebody who will.

Day 3
Give Him the Love He Needs

Loving your man isn't giving him a handie while he's driving. Loving your man isn't letting him bang you in the family bathroom at the movie theatre multiplex on date night! Loving your man isn't blowing him in your friend's bathroom during her cocktail party. And loving your man isn't waiting for him before he gets home from work in your super sexy lingerie with a cocktail in hand! Juuuuuuust kidding! It's all of those and then some. But most importantly, and all kidding aside, it's letting him vent from a long day. It's supporting the silliest of dreams he may have. It's respecting your man by always standing by him and challenging him in a way that makes him feel that you two are partners in this whole life thing. Tonight when he comes home, change into something sexy. Get out of those clothes you've been wearing all day and slip into a dress. Low cut top. Something you know he likes to see you in. And then, really ask him how his day was. Sit back and listen to this man you gave your life to.

Day 4
Hungry, but Not for Food

Feed your husband. Feed him meat, feed him snacks, feed the man beer! But did you know that's not all he's hungry for? I'm curious, ladies, as to when the last time you've *really* fed him? Spiritually. Emotionally. Logically. Men need to be challenged! Mentally! Don't let your guy walk in the door while you both just go along with your day-to-day dialogue. Feed his brain new information to make him a better man. Tonight, you will ask your man what his all-time favorite song is and why. After that, if you don't know already, ask him what his favorite movie is. While you're at it, ask him if he could be one person dead or alive, who would he be? Then tell him who you would be and why. Try it! You'll be astonished on what you learn about one another. And he'll be astonished that you even cared to ask.

Day 5
Give Pleasure

There is no such thing as overkill here. I just might mention this once or twice or 44 thousand times before we've concluded! What does "pleasured" mean to you? It may mean kind words, soft touch, gazing into your husband's eyes, and having him rub your feet. Well I have news for you. That is not, I repeat, NOT what men perceive as being pleasured. You know what your man likes (at least you better) and if you don't, find the fuck out, like right now! If you do, do it more. Then do it some more again. And just when you think you've pleasured him enough, pleasure him more. If you're not having sex with your husband, then you're spending way to much time with your AA vibrating companion! Aren't you attracted to him anymore? Or maybe you simply don't know how or don't remember how. Tomorrow morning, wake him up by doing what he likes. His day will be so much better for it and so will yours.

Day 6
Stop the Nagging

"Who meeeeeee? I never nag my husband!" "I never tell him what to do, or how to do it." "I never ask him to take out the trash or clean up the dog shit in the backyard as soon as he walks in the door from work." "In fact, insinuating that I'm a nag, is like calling me the 'C' word!" Well girls, if the shoe fits, wear it! Understand that nagging your husband is like telling him he's not good enough and that you don't trust him to have the common sense to do what needs to get done. In some cases though, yes, you married a dumbass that needs his hand held even while taking a piss. But the fact is this: You married a kind and honorable man that loves you and wants to show you his love by serving you. Trust your Prince Charming and he'll surprise you; nag him and he'll slowly die into submission and be your slave instead of your partner. You're in this together, so either lovingly tell him what needs to get accomplished if things aren't getting done, or simply zip it up and let him do things for himself. On this day, you must fight back the will to nag him to the point of him wanting to strangle himself with your long, giant tongue of death and destruction.

Day 7
Be Honest

Little untruths can go a long way and commonly begin with no ill intentions. They can start with little things like going to the grocery store and making a habit of getting cash back here and there and stashing it away; drinking a bottle of wine or two before anyone gets home for the day and mentioning no word about it; going someplace and meeting up with someone maybe you shouldn't be meeting with but making it more a part of your life. At the end of the day, if you're truly unhappy, be honest with your husband and tell him why. Men aren't all that smart sometimes, so we need you to spell it out. "I will divorce you if you can't change." It can be just that simple. Like any other normal human being, men can't read minds and pick up on hints you think you're being clear on. You want out? Tell him! You want him more than anything in the world? Tell him that, too. You both are meant to spend a loving lifetime together otherwise you wouldn't have married one another in the first place.

Day 8
TV Dinners vs. Chicken Pot Pie

A wise man I know once said that our lives should be less like TV dinners and more like pot pies. The way we behave and handle ourselves at work, school and home should be the same across the board. Webster's defines the term compartmentalize as 'the ability to separate into isolated compartments or categories.' It is unhealthy to separate and isolate different parts of your world from your husband's. Withholding information about your life from your spouse is untruthful and is in fact a lie. This is a great way to really fuck up your marriage. So, simply be honest with yourself and avoid this self-destruction before it's too late. On this day you need to make a choice: either discontinue your bad habits, or start planning the beginning to the end with your mate.

Day 9
Pay Attention to Him

Would you please get off your phone, computer, tablet or whatever is distracting you and pay the fuck attention to the life around you? It's helpful to be present for him and actually listen to what he's saying to you. Look into his eyes like you would a potential new boss while interviewing for a new job and actually listen. Your husband could have just asked you if he can buy you the beautiful Tiffany necklace you've been wanting for years, but you wouldn't have heard him because it's your turn to beat your opponent on your favorite Scrabble app! This is simple, and it's a two-way road. This morning, look into his eyes while he's talking and react and respond sincerely. It is awkward, especially if you're not use to doing so, but that's why you're reading this because you know that its time to get out of your comfort zone. You want to care and love him and grow old together.

Day 10
Finding the "You" When You First Met

A lot of this is trying to remember the passion, desire and intrigue you had when you first started realizing that this is the man you want to love and spend the rest of your life with. Do you remember when you two started dating? When he came to pick you up, would it be safe to say that you wanted to stun him with your beauty and doll yourself up? Of course you did. He loves that! Again girls, men are simple creatures and very much visual human beings. So work out a little and tone up; wear one of those sexy outfits he loves. Put on a little makeup for heaven sake, and try not to let yourself go. A little lipstick goes a long way. You want your man's eyes on you, not the other woman across the restaurant who's already figured this out!

Day 11
Give Him a Moment to Breathe

Think of your man as a smartphone. He's the music in your life, he makes you laugh, he makes you cry, he entertains you and he is that constant reminder of memories you've shared together. More than likely, you can't live without him; but also remember that constantly being all up in each other's face can take a toll on both of you. In essence, his battery can run low from time to time and needs a recharge. Sometimes a man just needs a few minutes, hours or even a day or two to regather himself. By allowing him to do so, you're letting him reflect, process and digest his life as it unfolds before him. So before you get all butt hurt because he needs a few moments to himself, realize he's doing it for you, your family and the well-being of those around him. When he comes home today, hand him a cold beer or favorite cocktail, and let him know without telling him that you'll give him a moment to wind down from his day.

Day 12
Be His Best Friend

What do you consider when you think of your best friend and the qualities of this person that attracts you to them? Do they make you laugh? Do they make you feel good about yourself? Do they comfort you when your little heart is hurting and bring over your favorite cocktail and movie on those not-so-great days? Do they know what really makes you tick? It's probably safe to say, ladies, that the answer would be HELL YES on all accounts, because our best friends are wonderful human beings and they fucking rock! I know you know where I'm going with this, so let's agree: It's probably advantageous to parallel those same qualities we love in others and mirror that into who you are to your husband. Are you doing this? If the answer is no, then HOLE-EE-SHIT! We've got some work to do! Take him out to a movie he's been looking forward to see tonight. Grab some Froyo on the way home and talk about the movie, life, and any random thing that comes to mind. Remember, you're best friends.

Day 13
Who's the Man?

If for one single nanosecond you thought to yourself that you're the man in the family when reading the title of this chapter, then you need to double check which one of you has the penis. Because it's sure as fuck not you, my dear; it's the man you married! No man on this planet wants to be emasculated by his girl. You might as well strip him down naked in the middle of the mall, crush his balls with your foot and spit on him. Harsh, right? Fuckin' A harsh! But that's what you're doing metaphorically. It's the little things that you may not even be aware of. Bragging on your friend's husband, going cray cray with your eyes (you just rolled your eyes after reading that), or simply being afraid of being too needy yet actually sincerely needing him. Compliment him today and be intentional on what you say, but more importantly, how you say it. Then seduce him, and give him no choice other then letting him show you his art of banging your brains out.

Day 14
Write Letters

A text in the middle of the day is nice. Love notes around the house are even better. But what tops the cake is a handwritten letter for him to see the words that are on your mind. He'll go back to it and read it over and over, and he'll keep it forever. It's these tiny little things that a man stores in his happy memory bank. Even more importantly now, is showing him what you wrote by applying it to your day-to-day lives. You love the way he smells? Curl up next to him and devour his scent. You like that he just got the promotion at work? Tell him you admire the fact that he earned the job because of how smart and savvy he is, along with knowing how much people respect him. It'll make him want to blow his new bonus all over you. It's the little things ladies that will slowly start moving the needle for you to get you out of the A-hole wife perception and back into the woman he fell for from the beginning. On this day, write him letter. Five sentences, one simple paragraph. I bet once you get started, you'll write more. He'll love it.

Day 15
Timing is Everything

As much as we'd love our marriages to live in perfect harmony with zero conflict and no disagreements, we all know that hell has a better chance of freezing over. So let's face it: Shit is going to go down sometimes. You're going to piss each other off. You must remember, however, that timing and tone is everything. When he walks in the door, give him a fucking second. Before you tell him how to fold towels the right way or that he left beard clippings in the sink this morning, let the man take a breather. You'll thank yourself later for letting him wind down. It could make all the difference in the world between talking like normal human beings with one another or yelling like crazy people.

Day 16
Eat His Heart Out

I'm sure you know that the quickest way into a man's heart is straight through his belly. Total cliché, right? Of course it is! It wouldn't be one if it wasn't completely true! More often than not, women are the main caregivers in feeding the family. So, keep up the good work, girls! For those women out there who can't tell the difference between a pot and a pan, it's probably about time to watch some YouTube and the Food Network or find a good take-out establishment that tastes and smells homemade. Not only do men love to be fed, they feel respected when being served upon. Serving your hubby is equivalent to you getting pampered while getting a mani/pedi. Pamper your man with a plethora of delicious recipes, and you will forever capture his heart. So what delicious dinner will you be making on Day 16? Maybe some Italian or Mexican dish to speak to his heart? You know his favorite, make that!

Day 17
Cry Me a River

Let's just get this out straight away: Crying is ok. Habitual crying…not so much. Men actually really aren't all that in love with crying. You leave him defenseless and give him no choice whatsoever of being the dipshit. How about that one time you had an issue with your husband? You started to cry when things weren't going your way. Guess what? You just screwed yourself out of that discussion! Your convo is over, and you put him in a non-win sitch. If he ignores your emotions, he's an insensitive asshat! It's all about the timing and balance of shedding a tear. Next time you feel compelled to cry but the timing or balance of the heated conversation isn't in your favor, finish the talk and then cry to the cat or a friend.

Day 18
Control by Giving Control

Did you know you're not very fun or pretty when you try to control every little fucking circumstance or situation? In fact, it's really annoying and shows that you have little to no faith in the choices and decisions your guy is making. It's time, girls, for you to pull up your stockings, get ready for a ride, and let him get back into the driver's seat. If your relationship isn't suffering already, then it will, and it just may be the season of your life to let go of this ugly trait and absorb the attribute of not undermining your better half in *every* life choice.

Day 19
The Strength of Touch

Saying something through touch can display many things: love, warmth, compassion and forgiveness. Who can't use some of that from time to time? A little goes a long way. Your man desires your touch and it makes him feel closer to you. When you wake up in the morning, scratch his arms with your new sexy manicure. Then move to his back. He won't stop you. Make your way down, and before long, he'll be purring like a Himalayan on catnip. It'll make him feel closer to you, and that's what he needs, wants and desires.

This is showing him you love him without saying a word.

Day 20
The Past is the Past

Remember that one time your hubby told you he was going to pick up the milk on his way home from work and forgot? Or that time when he threw his red t-shirt in the laundry when you were doing whites? Or that other time he came home an hour late to watch the kids, which made you late to go see Magic Mike 6 with your girlfriends? Here's what you do: From now on, when you aren't getting along, bring up every little time he fucked up and all his shortcomings to make him feel bad. Sound good? HELL NO that doesn't sound good! It's downright ridiculous. Don't make me sing you your favorite 'Frozen' song, but I will if I have to. Let it go! Drudging up the past is like rubbing your dog's face in a pee stain they made a month ago. It does zero good, it makes them feel awful, and they probably don't remember doing it anyway.

Day 21
STFU

You know what that means, right—STFU? Probably not, because you're always running your mouth and trying to be right. So, take it from me—please, **S**hut **T**he **F**uck **U**p! What? I said please! As I mentioned before, there's never a perfect marriage. You'll argue and you'll say things that you'll regret. So zip it up, and put a sock in it. No one has ever been wrong for being silent. Try it! Do him and you a favor, listen to him without having the answer already running in your head. You just might hear what he's actually trying to say to you.

Day 22
Wuv, Twue Wuv

Wuv, Twue Wuv! Isn't that all we need? Mostly, but did you know that everyone has a different love language? There are 5: Words of Affirmation, Acts of Service, Receiving Gifts, Quality Time and Physical Touch. Do you know yours? More importantly, do you know his? He may have all five in some sense. So, it may be time to get off your tablet, tell him you love him and cook his favorite dinner. Spoil his boxers right off him with some gifts, let him watch his favorite team that's on TV, and then after, lure him into your bedroom with those new high heels, thigh-high stockings and matching bra and underwear you just bought! Or, at least for starters, choose one.

Day 23
The Spice of His Life

You may be seeing a teeny tiny little pattern here that has been seasoned into a good majority of our day-to-day lessons. Men do love their seasoning. They love to season everything: their steak, their eggs, their chicken, their anything at any time! Alright, I'm not gonna beat around the bush here ladies because I'm pretty sure you know what we're getting at…SEX! It's SEX! Think of sex like seasons, the spice of life. Two things though, you very much need to know: men don't like asking for sex. If they're forced to seek the horizontal mambo by asking or hinting, gladly accept the majority of the time. A man getting rejected from sex is like someone asking you if you're pregnant, and you're not. It's awful, no fun and it makes you want to bang your head against the wall and knock yourself silly. Juuuuust kidding, but it does blow and not in a good way! This morning, afternoon or night (or all three for God's sake), go after your guy with a heat-seeking hunger that needs to be nourished! He needs it. You need it. Indulge. Repeat tomorrow.

Day 24
It's Never Nothing

Just like women have "women's intuition," men have a very scientific term for this too, it's called "Spidey Sense!" We know when you're pissed. We know when you're irritated. We know when we're not getting laid. In fact, we know a lot of unspoken shit that's going on in our lives, so pay attention to him when he feels that feeling. Here's the thing, if something is bothering you and he's concerned and asks, "What's wrong?" Tell him! Too commonly, women's go-to when being confronted with the question is, "Nothing." If the answer really *is* "Nothing," then wipe that sour look off you face that resembles Hillary Clinton after she realized why Monica Lewinsky always kept cigars at her desk. The fact is, when he senses something *is* wrong, something IS fucking wrong, because it's obvious! So, the next time he asks if everything is ok, either take acting classes to learn how to fool his Spidey Sense, or do the right thing, and just communicate with your man to remedy what's really on your mind.

Day 25
Give Him Praise

When was the last time you let your husband know what an amazing father he is, or how he touched on all the perfect spots while hiding the salami last night, or that the front and backyard lawn looks friggin' fantastic after working hard on a Saturday morning? Men love praise. We do! Praise to us guys is like cocaine and strippers to Charlie Sheen. Your man will adore you for giving him praise. It's the little things that go by unnoticed. It's super kick ass when these tiny things are recognized and brought to our attention by our beautiful and sexy brides. It makes us feel like a billion bucks. On this day, tell him whatever he did well, and creatively reward him for it.

Day 26
Kill That Green-Eyed Monster Called Jealousy

It's been said that trust is the cornerstone of the relationship. Let's face it girls, there are other women out there other than you. Your guy has no choice in the fact that he works with women, talks to women and sees women everywhere he goes. He may even be connected to a job where he works with absolutely drop dead gorgeous women. But you don't have to ever worry, because the love of your life chose you to journey life together. Comparing yourself to others needs to cease. Jealousy can turn the coolest people into crazy insane green-eyed monsters leaving zero sense for what's right or wrong. I get it, men need to have respect for their wives by not gawking or staring at other women, but the fact that he worked one-on-one with a stunning woman for weeks doesn't mean he was banging her in a hotel room. It's easy to concoct make believe scenarios in your mind that drive you mad or even into the arms of another man to get back at yours. That's when your marriage is officially over. Trust your husband, and trust what he says. And if he is truly happy with you and your marriage, he'll never want to be with anyone else.

Day 27
Roommates

Oftentimes when being married for quite a while, we forget that our spouse is our spouse, and all of a sudden you look across the dinner table and see a roommate. Do you hang out in different rooms? Can you remember when you had your last date? Are you still intimate or even having regular conversations? Do you sleep in separate beds? If the answer is yes to any of these, then you may, in fact, be living with a roommate instead of that man you chose over all the other men before him. You're reading this book because you want to change, and if you've come this far on Day 27, there's an excellent chance that you're a reasonable human being. On this day, preplan and find an awesome restaurant you both love and have wonderful conversations; take him somewhere to do something fun after dinner; then end the night with you on top of him in the bedroom pretending it's your first time together.

Day 28
Offer Support

Believe it or not, your man isn't perfect. In fact, he's beyond Captain Perfect and from time to time, he'll fuck up royally. On the job, raising the kids, maybe even the way he's treating you (he may need Book One in this series if he doesn't already have it), but accept that he will make mistakes. The focus here isn't how bad he made the mistake. The focus is how you react and respond to what happened. You may feel like this is the perfect time to criticize him and kick him while he's down for making a stupid decision. Actually, this is the time when he needs you the most to lend support in dealing with his shortcomings. Love him on this day, listen to him and help turn his mistake into an excellent growth opportunity for both of you.

Day 29
Be Who He Married

People marry one another because they are attracted to many things they see and experience with each other. They're attracted by their upbringing, spiritual beliefs, their sexiness, laugh, the way they smell, their love for movies and music, and their sense of humor. Be the person he married. That's all he ever wants. After a marriage sadly ends, one of the most common things people say is that, "people change." It's true, people do. However, it's advantageous to your marriage to change from a caterpillar to a butterfly instead of a caterpillar to a snake. Try to resemble who you once were and build on a better you from the person he fell in love with. Today, reflect on the person you were, and come up with ways to bring her back.

Day 30
When in Doubt

Holy shit! We did this! You got through all 30 days without throwing any dishes or pulling anybody's hair out. On this last day, I want you to remember one thing: When in doubt, refer back to Days 5 and 23! Along with that, be a trendsetter. Try new things and be the initiator—men love that! Take him in the car, take him in the family bathroom at the restaurant (they're private and the doors lock). How about relaxing your hand in his lap at a baseball game or at the movie theatre? Change it up, keep it interesting, and wear something so damn sexy that he won't be able to take his eyes off of you. Always leave him guessing when you're going to do the things he's always dreamed of!

Afterword:

Here's the deal: Marriage takes work. If you're not willing to work at it, I promise that you will live a miserable life. You've probably noticed by now, if you're making just a little effort and implementing the 30-day plan, you'll see drastic changes within yourself and in him. Has he begun to compliment you again and want to rub your feet after a long day? Has he brought a dozen roses home for you out of nowhere? If he hasn't, he will!

By now, you know you don't want to be an Asshole wife. And by now, you know how not to be one. We know deep down, REALLY deep down, that you're not an A-hole. If you really were, you wouldn't be reading this. So, come on back from time to time to this ridiculously easy 30-day guide, and brush up your skills. Rid yourself from being an A-hole wife, and more importantly, rid yourself of the possibilities of losing your husband forever.

Made in the USA
Monee, IL
10 November 2024

69776517R00039